M000023403

This Notebook Belongs To:

Made in United States
North Haven, CT
03 March 2023

33518650R00057